GO TEAM!
Mascots of the SEC

Delia Corrigan and Elizabeth Tighe

Go Team LLC
Columbia, South Carolina

Book design by Ashley Bowers

CHEERS FOR

Our MVPs:
Sam, Charlie, Edward, and Kevin; Margaret Anne, Mariah, Hagood, Robert Sims, and Hagood.

Special Teams:
Jason Ayer, John Bateman, Mary Lou Braswell, Sue Cate, Hen
Clay, Lyle Darnell, Jeanette Davis, Liz Demoran, Donnell Field,
Donni Frazier, Guy Gaster, Kent Gidley, Michael Gleason, Conn
Goldsmith, Erika Goodwin, Rhona Gray, Debbie Greenwell, Rus
Houston, Toni Karl, Van Kornegay, Amber Kosinsky, Eric Mirac
Carla J. Nail, George Newell, Braxton Newman, Pam Pearson, J
Postell, Brooke Pruitt, Victoria Reed, Mike Richey, Debbie Shaw
Justin Shugart, Jessica Smith, Amy Thames, Kathy Tidwell, Ji
Tran, Tammy Tucker, Lynn Welch, Pauline Zernott,
the spirit teams at each SEC college, the fabulous fans at tho
great schools, and especially to the wonderful mascots who
make us laugh and cheer.

ISBN 978-0-9797040-0-0
Library of Congress Control Number: 2008922869

Copyright 2008 by Delia Corrigan and Elizabeth Tighe.

First Edition. Printed in Korea.

A portion of the proceeds from the purchase of this book
goes to support Special Olympics.

STARTING LINE-UP

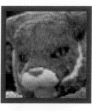

Whatever you do, do it all to the glory of God.
– I Corinthians 10:31

Albert

Gators
Home: Gainesville, Florida
School Colors: Orange and Blue
School founded in 1831

Warning! Don't Feed the Gators!
People take that caution seriously as they approach the huge orange wall beside Ben Hill Griffin Stadium in Gainesville, Florida. If there is any doubt whose territory it is, just look up and read the message... "This is *The Swamp*."

The University of Florida is home of the Gators — American gators, to be exact. These fierce reptiles bite harder than any other member of the animal kingdom and that is one reason Florida fans are quick to warn people, "Only Gators come out alive."

Young fans do not fear Albert the Alligator, Florida's seven-foot toothy mascot. He and his special friend, Alberta, are two of the friendliest alligators around. And boy, are they around! They nest in Lake Alice, enjoy the Okefenokee Swamp and, on game day, Albert moves around in The Swamp with 90,000 other Gators.

"When you hear fans telling each other to meet at 'Albert and Alberta,' they are talking about our bronze statue in the Gator Club Plaza," says Albert. "It was a gift from some of the students, and you should see it. It looks just like us." The statue shows the two of them holding hands, and it is true that they fancy each other. Alberta looks pretty in her orange cheerleading uniform and bow, and Albert is dapper in his hat and sweater.

The couple is often together on the University of Florida campus for special events, such as Big Gator/

Little Gator Day. This is a day when area school children come to college to see what university life is like. In addition to going to classes and eating with a university student, these lucky Gators get to hug Albert and Alberta. "I love to hug the children, and I also like to rub their heads. Sometimes this surprises them, but it always makes them smile," says Albert.

Albert and Alberta frequently wade into town to eyeball things and, like many American Alligators, people find them in surprising places. Since Albert loves celebrating people's birthdays, he is always ready for a party. Albert points to a picture. "This is a photo of a 95-year-old birthday boy running a race. Look, I'm right beside him! I'll never forget that day."

At a Memory Walk event for Alzheimer's disease, fans spot Albert and Alberta waving from the back of a firetruck. On another day, Albert chomped and cheered for a girl who won her race at the Special Olympics. "When she came up to me and said, 'I did it! Albert, I won!' I forgot my tough side and shed a joyful alligator tear."

Albert and Alberta care about their state and their habitat, and sometimes this takes them to other parts of Florida. Albert remembers a special time when they made a trip to the state capitol in Tallahassee to talk about the important Okefenokee Swamp. "I sensed there was a birthday boy around, so I followed my nose right into the governor's office birthday party. I enjoyed a little cake and gave the governor a nice rub on his head," says Albert.

Albert is at all the University of Florida athletic games, and travels anywhere there is Florida football and basketball. "I go to areas that are not indigenous to alligator life and feast on such delicacies as bulldogs, wildcats, gamecocks, and tigers," Albert says. Alberta enjoys watching all of the women's athletic events, so she is a regular in the crowd or on the sidelines.

One of the highlights of the year is homecoming week. The week begins with the Sun Trust Gator Gallop, and those who'd rather wear skates can participate in the Gator Skater. On Friday night before the homecoming game, Gator Growl takes place. This is the largest pep rally in the world, and the University of Florida mascots are lucky they always get to participate, because the tickets get sold out fast. "There is great entertainment, and I help get the Gator fans fired up. My tail swishes just thinking

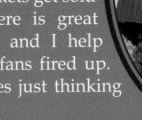

about all that blue and orange."

Albert has a hero and sometimes even dresses like him. "My hero's name is Mr. Two Bits. For more than 50 years he moved around the stadium leading the fans in cheers for the Gators. Mr. Two Bits started the tradition when he noticed some people booing instead of cheering, and he decided to show them a better way to support the team," says Albert. At every game Mr. Two Bits wore the same thing as he did on that first day, so if you see Albert take off his orange t-shirt and put on gray pants, a yellow shirt, and an orange and blue tie, you'll know why. He is dressing like his hero, Mr. Two Bits.

"Even in a swampy habitat," Albert says, "good sportsmanship is important. So let's hear it! Two bits, four bits, six bits, a dollar! All for the Gators, stand up and holler!"

Mascot Message

Always show good sportsmanship
It's fun to do special things for others

9

Aubie

Tigers
Home: Auburn, Alabama
School Colors: Orange and Blue
School founded in 1856

Aubie the Tiger raises his arms and swings his tail. He jokes with band members and poses with fans for photographs. "It's great to be an Auburn Tiger, and it is wonderful to be the mascot," says Aubie, the Tiger with attitude.

Aubie stretches out in the sun by Sewell Hall. "One of my favorite Auburn traditions is the Tiger Walk.

Two hours before the game, fans line up right here and walk to the stadium with the football team. For about one-and-a-half miles, the path is packed with crowds on both sides. The players wear their dress-up clothes and I wear

my blue jersey. Of course, I stride along with them to make sure everyone is excited about the game. Occasionally I share a few of my ambush strategies with the coach," says Aubie.

Aubie is on the prowl at all Auburn sports events, sometimes in the stands and other times with the band or cheerleaders. During basketball games he darts out to participate in the cheers or chase away the opposing mascot.

Tailgating at the Alumni Tent is an Auburn tradition that Aubie won't miss. "Yum! Gator tail—my favorite," says Aubie. He gives plenty of hugs and handshakes to his fans, big and small. Aubie also hangs out at the Tiger Team Village, where kids play games. "Hey, look at this!" shouts a little girl. "It's Aubie's paw print! He gave me his autograph!"

Even though Aubie the Tiger keeps busy at

many Auburn athletic events, he makes special time for visits in the community. "I just returned from the Children's Hospital, where I passed out some of my wonderful calendars. Did you know I am featured on a calendar every year?" asks Aubie.

Why did the Auburn fans and students choose a tiger for their mascot? The answer comes from a line in a poem written in 1770 by Oliver Goldsmith. The people of Auburn agree with Goldsmith's description that Auburn is the "loveliest village on the plain." They also believe another line in the poem describes their ferocious athletic teams: "Where crouching tigers wait their hapless prey."

Aubie's life began on the cover of Auburn football programs. "I found it to be a little flat, if you know what I mean. When I finally decided to spring to action it was an incredible feeling. I love the smiles on everyone's faces as I make my appearances," says Aubie.

Aubie sure did smile when he was the first college

mascot inducted into the Mascot Hall of Fame. "That is one of my favorite memories, and I will always cherish the award. It's not every day you can say you were the first to do or be something."

Aubie's mascot fame has spread far and wide, so many people wonder why Auburn University has a live golden eagle that lives in his aviary next to Jordan–Hare Stadium. Aubie explains, "We have a special eagle because we have a special battle cry— 'War Eagle!'

"When it was time to name our eagle, people couldn't get me out of their minds, so they named him Tiger. So I'm Aubie the Tiger, and he's Tiger the eagle. Simple!" Aubie purrs as he takes a satisfying tiger stretch.

Tiger is a rare golden eagle; since the early 1930s Auburn fans have believed he brings good luck. For more than 40 years, students from Alpha Phi Omega fraternity had the important job of caring for the eagle. Now Tiger is under the protection of the Southeastern Raptor Rehabilitation Center. Fans visit Tiger in his aviary, or look for him before and after football games.

Aubie loves to watch Tiger, especially when he

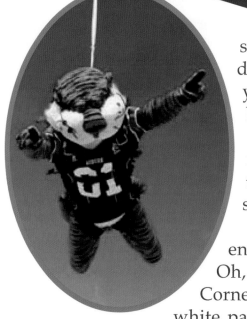

swoops down to the 50-yard line for a closer look before the game. One day Aubie decided it must feel great to move through the air like that, so he learned to skydive!

"From the sky I see the entire beautiful campus. Oh, look—there's Toomer's Corner, and I can see some white paper hanging in the oak tree. It must still be there from the last victory celebration, when fans decorated the trees with toilet paper. I think I'll land and have some lemonade at Toomer's Drugs," says Aubie.

Aubie is one of a kind and he likes it that way. "I'm often imitated, but never duplicated," says Aubie. As he pads back to his den under Jordan–Hare Stadium, he says in a satisfied growl, "There is a popular saying about me here on campus. 'The women love me and the men want to be like me.' **Grrrrrrrrrrrr! War Eagle!"**

Mascot Message

It's fun to try new things
Tigers are never scared

Big Al

Red Elephants
Home: Tuscaloosa, Alabama
School Colors: Crimson and White
School founded in 1831

At the University of Alabama, a distant rumble grows louder and louder. Trumpets blare like elephants and out stomps the crimson and white Alabama football team. Leading the herd is Big Al, the mascot for the Alabama Red Elephants.

Big Al says, "Many years ago, students here at the University of Alabama decided they

wanted me to be part of their spirit team. I've been showing up ever since!"

Elephants are the largest land mammal and can be very fierce at times, so it is easy to be a little afraid when you are around one. But when fans see how cheerful and silly Big Al is, there is no doubt he is a unique elephant. "They say I'm cuddly and lovable, and they're right!" Big Al rumbles at a low frequency.

Big Al likes to eat tree bark, fruit, grass and leaves. His favorite snack is peanuts. Sometimes Big Al carries a bag of them around during a game. "If I run out of peanuts I look around to see if a fan will share with me," Big Al says as he plunges his trunk into the bag again.

Big Al loves school. "My best subject is P.E. and my hardest subject is handwriting. I think it's funny that I have an easy time knocking down a tree, but a hard time holding a pencil," Al says with a big gray grin. "But good writing is very important. In fact, I wouldn't be the Bama mascot if it weren't for the words of a very good writer."

What could Big Al mean? He must be talking about the time a sports writer compared the huge Alabama football players to a herd of elephants charging down the field. The Alabama fans liked that description so much that they made Big Al the official mascot.

"That's not the only time a good written description of our team has led to a lasting tradition," says Al. "Have you ever heard us yell 'Roll Tide Roll'?" Al gladly explains.

"In 1907, we were playing a football game against Auburn. The Auburn Tigers were favored to win that year. Well," continues Al, "it had rained and rained, and the whole football field was slippery with red mud. It was hard for the players to move forward even an inch without getting stuck in the muck.

"Do you think the Alabama players gave up? No! They kept fighting and pushing, and a sports writer wrote that they were like an ocean tide that just kept coming forward, little by little. They held Auburn to a 6-6 tie and did not lose the game after all. Everyone liked that description of our team being like a red ocean tide, and now we are known as the Crimson Tide."

Big Al loves birth-
day parties, play-
grounds and other
fun community
events. On game
day, he rides in the
Rammer-Jammer
to the quad. He
gets down on his
knee and shakes
hands with the
fans, and then he
leads the cheer-
leaders in a parade
to the stadium.

Big Al has a quick
dust bath and he is
ready for the
"Bama Spell-Out." "This is my favorite cheer!" he
says. With the help of the Million Dollar Band, he
leads the fans and the cheerleaders as everyone
spells out each letter in the word A-L-A-B-A-M-A!
Each time they shout "A!" Big Al pokes out his
round tummy so everyone can see the "A" he
proudly wears on his red shirt. The cheer ends with
the popular shout, "Roll Tide Roll!" as Al rolls his
whole belly around and around.

"When something exciting is happening, I look for
a big tree trunk or a goal post to knock down.
Usually I get the team flag instead, and run around
for a while," says Al.

Al is usually a happy elephant, but there have been times that he has been a little sad. Al says, "I remember one time a person in the crowd squirted me with a water hose. For a moment I wanted to use my long trunk to squirt him back, even harder than he squirted me. But then I decided a better idea was to avoid that person. I stayed real close to my friends and before long I felt much better."

Al also gets sad when people pull hard on his trunk. "My trunk is important because I use it for breathing, feeding, washing, drinking, and communicating." If you watch closely you may see Al swing his trunk back and forth, twirl it like a propeller or even hug his trunk for comfort.

"Did I tell you that I love P.E.?" Al asks. "When my teachers hand out hula-hoops, I blare with excitement. I am really good at it, because I just roll my belly and think, 'Roll Tide Roll!'"

Big Red

Razorbacks
Home: Fayetteville, Arkansas
School Colors: Cardinal and White
School founded in 1871

"Woooooooooooooooo, Pig! Sooie!"
The call goes out all over Arkansas. No matter what the sport, the University of Arkansas Razorback mascot family is there. That's right, it's a family thing for the hogs. Big Red, the original mascot, introduces his kin. "Look up and you'll see Boss Hog. And these little tykes are Pork Chop and Sue E."

A razorback is a ferocious hog with a ridge of hair that stands up along its back. They live in the southeastern

United States. Big Red explains, "We're feral hogs. That means we can't be tamed. We remain wild at all times." No wonder there are "Beware of Hogs" signs all over Arkansas.

Big Red's large tusks and fierce eyes are intimidating. Often children keep their distance because it is clear he means business. Luckily, Pork Chop, Sue E and Boss Hog are always ready to play.

Pork Chop is a piglet who loves children. He hugs, waves and motions kids to follow him. Sometimes he gets into trouble. "I'm so busy playing that I forget where I am," giggles Pork Chop. You might see him near the scoreboard or far away in the crowd. "When I get separated from Sue E, I become a little afraid, so I go back to where she is," he says.

Sue E is important to the Arkansas effort. She prances over to her wooden closet. "Everyone will be watching me, especially when I dance. What should I wear? I have overalls, homecoming gowns and a Santa suit, just to name a few," says Sue E. "I often put on my cheerleading uniform so I look official while I cheer for the team. They count on me."

You can't miss the nine-foot-tall inflatable razorback named Boss Hog. He jumps, dances and moves in surprising ways. "I am very good at skipping and touching my toes. During half-time, the crowd cheers as I put on a show. The only thing that stops me is when I have to chase off the other team's mascot,"

Boss Hog oinks proudly. Even during a chase, he never stops smiling.

Fans can see the mascots before home football games at a big tent called the "Trough." Many fans eat barbecue or bacon because they believe it will bring good luck to their team.

Another favorite place the Razorback family likes to go is the Road Hog area, where many alumni park their RVs. Sometimes those fans stay all week! Here you can see Tusk, a live 380-pound hog. You might catch the cheerleaders riding on top of his cage.

"I get so excited to see the team," squeals Sue E. "We greet the players when they get off the bus at the stadium."

Pork Chop adds, "I love it when the sports announcer, the Voice of the Hogs, yells, 'Let's call those hogs!' Then Reynolds Razorback Stadium shakes as fans call their favorite hogs by shouting, 'Woooooooooo, Pig, Sooie!'"

Everyone is hog wild about the Razorback Marching Band. Begun in 1874, it is one of the oldest college bands in the country. Before the game, the Marching Razorbacks form an 'A' the length of the football field. While the band plays, the team, coaches and spirit squad run out on the field. "I run through the 'A' carrying our large flag and join my family in the middle of the field," says Big Red.

"Hog calls, Road Hogs and running through the 'A' are just some of our Arkansas traditions," Big Red continues. "Let me show you another one. Here's a hint… you have to look down." The mascots trot to Old Main, the oldest building on campus. Pointing at the sidewalk, Big Red starts reading names. What in hognation is he doing? Sue E explains, "This is where Senior Walk begins. The name of every senior is

stamped on the walkway that winds through the school. There are over 120,000 names on the sidewalk. It goes on for five miles!"

Plopping down in a big pig pile, the hogs admit being a mascot is not always easy. Pork Chop says, "Once I fell down and the crowd laughed. Instead of getting mad, I decided to laugh with them." Big Red remembers the time he carried the flag out of the tunnel. Instead of waving nicely, it twisted up. "I had to get over it, move on and do it right the next time," Big Red grunts.

"I can't seem to recall making any mistakes," says Sue E with a delicate snort.

Big Red, Pork Chop, Sue E and Boss Hog are a great mascot family. They work together to cheer for the Razorbacks. Sometimes fans have a hard time deciding what to watch — the game or the mascots!

Mascot Message

Learn to laugh at your mistakes
Families support each other and work together

Bully

Bulldogs
Home: Starkville, Mississippi
School Colors: Maroon and White
School founded in 1878

In 1905, a few days after Thanksgiving, Sam Allen leaped off the white wooden porch of his home in Starkville, Mississippi and headed downtown to fetch a newspaper for his father. He pulled his flat wool cap down close to his ears as the coins Papa gave him jingled in the pocket of his brown knickers. Before he could finish whistling "Camptown Racetrack," Sam reached Main Street

MISSISSIPPI STATE UNIVERSITY

and hopped up onto the broad boardwalk
that lined it. He spied Charlie up ahead.

"Hey, Charlie! My Pop sent me out for a paper. You
heard anything about the big game?"

"Sam! Can you believe it? The Bulldogs did it!
They shut out Ole Miss 11 to nothin'."

"Gee, I wish I coulda' seen it. I bet it was a great
game. Say — what's that noise? It sounds like horns
and trumpets. Is there a band playing?" Startled, the
boys looked around.

"Let's go, Sam. It's comin' from over there," said
Charlie. The boys raced off to Capitol Street.

A strange parade led by a brass band was passing.
Students from Mississippi State University were
playing the instruments. Instead of a happy tune,
they were playing a dreary funeral march. The boys
stared as another group of students walked behind
the band carrying a coffin draped in red and blue.
Looking closer, they saw a small bulldog puppy riding on top of the coffin.

"Lookit, Sam, it's a crazy prank! Those guys have

decorated up
a coffin in
Ole Miss col-
ors and put
that bulldog
on top 'cause
they killed
'em today on
the football
field!"

Everybody cheered wildly. What a great day for the Bulldogs.

The year has changed but MSU fans still celebrate every win by their teams wearing maroon and white. Their athletes have always been tenacious and tough, just like the real live bull-dogs that are kept on campus. In 1961, the English Bulldog became the school's official mascot. Bully is a real dog who lives at the University School of Veterinary Medicine when he is not on duty at home football games.

Bully is also the name of the life-size bulldog mascot who appears at all the different athletic events to entertain the crowd. How does he get ready for a football game? "Dogs like to snooze, but on game day I have to get up and running. To start my day off, I have my favorite food—a big juicy steak! I go to several pep rallies then I get my doghouse ready because I ride on top of it to the game." During the games at Davis Wade Stadium, he trots up and down the sidelines helping the cheerleaders spark the crowd.

Bully loves exciting the fans because it encourages

the team. "The athletes work even harder to win when they can tell the crowd is behind them. It's tough when they lose because it disappoints everybody." But Bully doesn't run away with his tail between his legs after a loss. "No way!" he barks. "We learn from the mistakes so we can win next time."

Being a mascot is hot work and Bully gets dog tired. "Instead of sweating as people do, I pant to keep cool. I keep a towel nearby to mop my jowls, and I pop into my doghouse to cool off with some water from my bowl," explains Bully.

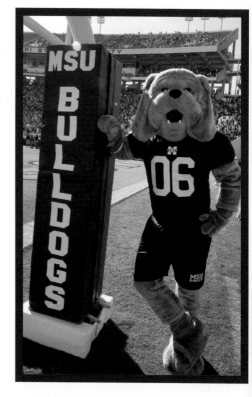

When Bully is feeling frisky, he loves dancing to his favorite song by Chuck Smooth. He even howls along with it... "Who let the dogs out... whoo! whoo! whoo!... Who let the dogs out?" He is not a great singer but it is doggone funny to hear him howl to the beat.

Dogs crave attention so Bully never gets embarrassed when he

is clowning around for the crowd. He loves it when children give him a pat. English Bulldogs look a little scary but Bully is as gentle as a lamb. The term "bulldog" describes how this dog breed looks like a small bull. Also, during the middle ages, these dogs were traind to attack bulls in arenas. "Nah, I don't want to attack any live bulls. But I will gladly go after Rebels, tigers and other wild animals," says Bully.

Bully loves school. "I can't get enough of it. I've been going for more than 15 years. If I'm not sniffing out trouble, I have my nose in a good book. *Old Yeller* is my favorite."

After a big game, Bully curls up for a good nap. His wrinkly face opens up with a big yawn as he puts his massive head down and snores. He dreams happily about a perfect world where everyone wears maroon and white, every meal is a thick steak and MSU beats Ole Miss every time.

Mascot Message

Learn from your mistakes
Never underestimate the power of the mascot

Cocky

Fighting Gamecocks
Home: Columbia, South Carolina
School Colors: Garnet and Black
School founded in 1801

As people grab a program and take their seats at Williams–Brice Stadium in Columbia, South Carolina, a young fan asks, "What is that big black box doing down on the football field?" That's a good question.

A few minutes before kick-off, all eyes stare at the mysterious box as the cheering becomes louder and louder. The low beat of the kettle drums and the blare of the brass instruments make 83,000 spines tingle as the thrilling theme song from the movie "2001 — A Space Odyssey" fills everyone's ears. A cock crows, and a loud crack startles the crowd as smoke surrounds the magic black box. Out

pops Cocky in all his red-feathered glory! With a white-gloved "thumbs up" for all the fans, he cheers on the Gamecocks and entertains the crowd. The Gamecock football team runs onto the field, and there is no doubt that they are ready to play. Cocky will be there the whole game, dancing and cheering, and helping the crowd pull for the team.

Before the game begins, Cocky rides to the stadium in a convertible. He arrives in plenty of time to tailgate and peck at some food. "Rooting for my favorite people in the warm climate of South Carolina takes loads of energy." Cocky covers his top beak with his hand and laughs when he's asked what his favorite food is. "Anything but chicken!" he clucks.

Sometimes on game day Cocky follows the tracks to the Cockaboose Railroad, which is an old railroad track right in the shadow of Williams–Brice Stadium. He knows that inside the restored cabooses, he'll find lots of serious tailgaters who are ready to cheer on the Gamecocks. He also visits with the live garnet and black gamecock, who perches on his very own goalpost, keeping an eye on the action.

Fans who want to see Cocky can go to more than football and basketball games. If the Gamecocks are playing, Cocky is there. "Sometimes supporters are surprised to see me at track-and-field meets," says Cocky. "But I can't sit in my roost knowing the Gamecock athletes are out there trying their hardest to bring home the victory," he says with a flourish of his red wing. "And after the contest, if the Gamecocks have won I couldn't be happier. If they lose, I want to be near them to remind them to keep trying, because there's always another chance!"

Cocky's mother and father are proud of him. His daddy, Big Spur, was the school mascot before Cocky. Big Spur taught Cocky many important things about being a mascot, and Cocky has used that training to develop into a champion.

"Have you seen me lead my favorite cheer?" Cocky asks. "It's the 'Shake a Tail

Feather Dance,' which was written with me in mind. And if you're wondering," Cocky adds, "gamecocks can't fly but I've still got serious 'ups'! When the cheerleaers form a pyramid, they make me feel as though I'm flying as they hold my legs and lift me to the top."

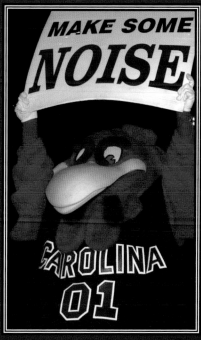

During Parents' Weekend, his Mom and Dad come to the game to watch him. "That's my boy!" clucks Big Spur as he puffs up and watches Cocky conduct the USC band just as he did when he was young. Cocky also feels his Dad's presence at the Colonial Center where the Gamecocks play basketball. This is because there is a mosaic of Big Spur on the floor at the main entrance. Cocky points to the floor and explains, "A mosaic is a picture made up of lots of pieces of stone. Sometimes after the fans and I play 'Find Cocky with the Spotlight,' I run in my basketball shoes to take a peek at Dad's mosaic. It reminds me of

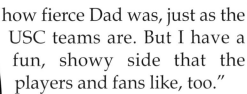

how fierce Dad was, just as the USC teams are. But I have a fun, showy side that the players and fans like, too."

What kind of a mascot is a gamecock? Gamecocks are roosters specially bred to fight. They are tough, ferocious and fight to the death. Today, because of its violence and cruelty, gamecock fights are illegal. But for many years, watching gamecock fights was a popular sport. Even the ancient Greeks participated in cockfighting.

There's another reason the people of USC chose the gamecock as their mascot. Thomas Sumter, a South Carolinian, was a hero of the Revolutionary War. During the Battle of Kings Mountain, which was an important Patriot victory in the war, he fought so courageously that the British officers who were trying to catch him said he "fought like a gamecock."

Since 1903, the Gamecock has been the mascot of the University of South Carolina. Cocky reminds everyone, "Lots of teams have tigers for their mascots, lots of teams have dogs. But there's only one SEC Fighting Gamecock, and that's me! **Go Cocks!**"

Mascot Message

Shake hands after every game, win or lose
Play fair and have fun

Colonel
.... Reb

Rebels
Home: Oxford, Mississippi
School Colors: Cardinal Red and Navy Blue
School founded in 1848

Colonel Reb sits on his porch and smiles. "Yessiree, it's great being the mascot at the University of Mississippi," he says as he gently rocks in his wooden rocking chair. "There's nothing better than the Grove on a bright clear day and some Ole Miss athletes giving their best to win it for the University."

Why is the University of Mississippi called Ole Miss? "Back in 1896, the school had a contest to pick a name for the yearbook. 'Ole Miss' won. Over time, it became a nickname for the school." So how did the school get the Rebel as their mascot? "Why, we had another contest, of course," chuckles the Colonel. "Around 1936, the school newspaper, *The Daily Mississippian*, sent ballots to Southern sports writers and they voted for the Rebels. The school adopted the name and we've been the Ole Miss Rebels ever since."

The Grove is the heart of Ole Miss. A ten-acre park in the center of campus, the Grove is the only place to be on a football Saturday. Colonel Reb describes the Grove. "On game days, the Grove is closed off for tailgating. Cars aren't allowed, so people bring in tables and tents. But this isn't tailgating as most folks think about tailgating. It is fancy with table-cloths and flowers, fried chicken and deviled eggs, and everybody all dressed up for a garden party.

Some tents have iron chandeliers hanging in them! Young'uns toss footballs and pretty girls smile at the fellers in their coats and ties."

Two hours before kick-off, the football team walks to Vaught-Hemingway Stadium through the Grove. After they pass through the Walk of Champions Arch, fans line the walkway and clap as the team passes by. The brick-and-iron Arch was donated by the 1962 team which was the only team in Ole Miss history to go undefeated (10–0). Colonel Reb loved walking with the team and the coaches to the stadium.

Colonel Reb continues, "After the game, folks hang around the Grove, swapping stories and eating. The University's Pride of the South Band gathers and performs crowd favorites. Little kids are tired and muddy, but keep right on playing and tossing foot-balls. Some even have those balls that glow in the dark."

"Children used to be able to climb the large oak

trees in the Grove, but not anymore. They worry somebody will fall out of one and get hurt. The trees tower over everything, providing soft shade as the day ends," says Colonel Reb.

"Life moves a little slower the rest of the week. Often, I head over to Square Books, a terrific bookstore. I climb the creaky stairs to the second floor to get an ice cream cone or a fancy coffee. Then I pass the time sitting on the porch. I look over the newspaper headlines, or settle in for a good read. You know, I bought *Where the Red Fern Grows* there. It's one of my favorites!"

Speaking of red, where did those school colors of red and blue come from? "Why, of course we had a contest!" jokes the Colonel. "Nope, I'm pullin' your leg. The team manager thought the crimson of

Harvard and the navy blue of Yale would go well together, and it would be good to have the spirit of both schools. I like it that those two wonderful colleges were an inspiration for Ole Miss."

Colonel Reb continues, "It is important for everyone to have positive role models. When I perform my duties as the mascot, I am well aware that lots of people are watching me and that plenty of those eyes belong to children." The Colonel says, "I try hard to always be a credit to Ole Miss."

Is there anything scary about being the mascot? "In my much younger days, I would rappel from the ceiling of the basketball arena to center court! Rappel means to go down something steep by using a rope that is attached at the top. The other end of the rope is passed through a harness that you wear. It is sort of like rock climbing. My army training sure came in handy then. It was a right scary stunt. I had much more fun shooting free throws at halftime with the cheerleaders."

Will he ever leave Ole Miss? "Lawsy," laughs Colonel Reb. "As we say, you may graduate from the University, but you never graduate from Ole Miss!"

Mascot Message

Find some good role models
Be respectful of your elders

Hairy Dawg

Bulldogs
Home: Athens, Georgia
School Colors: Red and Black
School founded in 1785

"We're going to the Sugar Bowl!" The cry went out all over Georgia, as the Bulldogs got ready to face Notre Dame in New Orleans. The year was 1980, and Coach Vince Dooley wanted the perfect mascot to help them win the game.

Since 1956, Uga, an English screwtail bulldog, has slobberingly graced the sidelines of Sanford Stadium in his red Georgia shirt. He is one of the few lucky creatures allowed to loiter "between the hedges," as Georgia fans say.

Though Uga is the most-loved bulldog in Georgia, before that Sugar

Bowl game the Georgia Athletic Department asked another dog, Hairy Dawg, for mascot help. "I have always loved the Georgia Bulldogs, so I left my bone behind and jumped into the silver britches they gave me," says Hairy Dawg. "I've been the Georgia mascot ever since!"

Like most faithful dogs, once Hairy Dawg was allowed to be a part of the action, nothing could keep him away. He showed up at Sanford Stadium the following year at the first home game. The Bulldogs won again, this time against a tough Tennessee team. Mascot Hairy Dawg was there to stay.

At every home game Hairy Dawg is dressed out in his football uniform, striding up and down the sidelines as he pays close canine attention to the plays and the fans. He sniffs out a spot near the cheerleaders, the Redcoat Marching Band, a doghouse and a fire hydrant. And, of course, near Uga.

Do the two mascots ever feel jealous of each other? "No!" answers Hairy Dawg. "Uga is my best friend and, like everyone else, he loves me. We wrestle around with one another during the games. Once he bit the fool out of my paw but it's all in good fun."

Hairy has tried to wriggle into Uga's air conditioned dog house on some of those dog days of

summer, but there was just not enough room for the two of them.

"That's Uga's house. Even though the heat is hard for me with all my fur, I've never been very good at the 'sit!' command. Especially when the Dawgs are playing," says Hairy Dawg.

"Recently, I had fun frisking with the fans. They lifted me up and we did a little crowd surfing. I could tell Uga wanted to stay right where he was."

All Georgia athletics make Hairy Dawg drool. Hairy says, "I try to attend at least one of each type of athletic event during the year. When I show up at equestrian meets to watch the horses, I keep my distance so they won't get skittish." Fans spot him at hundreds of other school and community affairs each year, but Hairy doggedly insists, "My main duties are football in the fall and basketball in the winter."

His spiky collar, huge jaws and fierce eyes can be scary, and his big strut in his athletic uniform leaves no doubt that he can sniff out a Bulldog victory. "I have been described as intimidating, and *Muscle and Fitness* magazine named me the buffest mascot of the SEC," Hairy says. "I use my muscles to pump up the crowd and showcase my dancing skills. Want a demonstration?" Hairy Dawg asks.

Besides lapping up lots of water, Hairy Dawg regularly chews on gator tails. "If I have to go a season without them, the flavor is even better when it is time to 'Let the big dog eat!'"

On a home football game day, Hairy Dawg's tail is thumping as he jumps into the cheerleaders' pick-up truck. Hairy makes the #1 sign and raises his paws in the air for high fives. "After a pep rally with the Motor Coach Club, we make our way to the Dawg Walk, where the players walk in," says Hairy. "The Redcoat Marching Band plays my favorite songs, like 'Glory, Glory,' and we all talk about how it's 'Great to be a Georgia Bulldog!'"

After a victory, Hairy Dawg races to the

Chapel to hear the beautiful sound of the chapel bell ringing. Sometimes he gets a chance to ring the bell, an old tradition on the Georgia campus that lets everyone know that the Dawgs have won.

After all the excitement, Hairy Dawg is tired. He pauses for a few minutes near the main gate, in front of the first Uga's grave. "Once Uga I retired, he passed the honor to his offspring, and that tradition continues to this day," says Hairy Dawg.

The muscles in Hairy's body are taut and his ears stand up as he recalls the crowd chanting, "Go Dawgs! Sic 'em! Woof! Woof! Woof!" His duties are done for the day and, like most dogs, he spends his spare time relaxing, dreaming of the next Georgia victory.

Mascot Message

It's great to be yourself
Keep that attitude positive

Mike

Tigers
Home: Baton Rouge, Louisiana
School Colors: Purple and Gold
School founded in 1860

Have you ever heard a tiger roar, *really* roar? On game days in Baton Rouge, Louisiana, tiger sounds come from above, below and basically anywhere there are Louisiana State fans. People have growling contests. The mascot, Mike the Tiger, stands by a cage while a real live Bengal tiger opens his huge jaws and roars at the opposing team. Fans believe that the

number of roars will equal the number of touchdowns that day, so they want him to shout! Why all this noise? Well, of course it is because LSU is the proud home of the Fighting Tigers.

Mike the Tiger says, "I was born in 1896 right after a perfect football season. My fans named me after a battalion of brave Civil War veterans from our state. They fought with such courage at the Battle of Shenandoah that they were nicknamed 'The Fighting Band of Tigers.'

"Our actual live tiger is very scary," says Mike, "so I am here to be the friendly tiger. I am pals with Mike, the Bengal tiger, but he is so dangerous he stays in his cage, while I get to run and play. And don't worry—his habitat is the biggest and best in the United States, and he loves it."

Before football games, the live tiger rides around Tiger Stadium in a portable cage as the cheerleaders bravely ride on top. He likes to stop for a while near the opposing team's locker room. Mike the Tiger says,

"I know I'm fearless and everything, but I wouldn't want to be on the other team when they have to pass that cage to get to the field. Yikes!"

What does Mike the Tiger like to eat? "Well, I love the Cajun food here in Louisiana. Sometimes I stride along the huge, beautiful live oaks on our campus until I find people who have some of my favorites such as hot boudin, jambalaya and my very favorite, fried alligator.

"Another thing I like to do is listen to special words and music that have been in our Louisiana culture ever since French settlers came here long ago. My favorite Cajun word is geaux — you know, like 'Geaux' Tigers!" says Mike.

"People say I'm a bit of a show-off, but I can't help

it. I love to spin around and perform in front of a crowd. I joined a headstand contest once, but a little girl beat me fair and square by standing on her head the longest."

Usually Mike the Tiger wears a

team jersey. Sometimes he puts his very own tiger-sized Mardi Gras beads around his neck. "One of the most famous Mardi Gras celebrations is here in Louisiana, in the city of New Orleans," boasts Mike. "There are parades, floats, costumes, and lots and lots of Tiger fans!"

Mardi Gras is a festival that was brought to Louisiana by French explorers. They were used to celebrating the festival in their homeland, and decided to continue their tradition. "Right," says Mike. "I jump up on a float and toss candy and beads to the kids. It just wouldn't be the same if I didn't join in the celebration."

At basketball games, Mike the Tiger spots the young fans. "I hang out at the Kidzone, behind the goal. I love to see them cheering on the Tigers. From time to time I throw candy, and the kids jump and reach for it," says Mike.

Mike the Tiger often swings his tail around and around. Could this be a nervous habit? "Tigers are never scared. This tail is handy for my dance moves and to twirl when it's a close game," says Mike. Maybe he does get a little nervous!

Mike loves to dance to the beat of the Golden Band from Tigerland. When he hears the band begin to play the song, 'Hey Fighting Tiger,' Mike's muscles are taut and ready. Cartwheels, dancing, running, jumping, and twirling are just a few of his moves. "Anytime the Tigers win is great," Mike the Tiger says. "If we happen to lose, I go visit Mike the live tiger at his home. We pace back and forth, and think about how we can play better next time.

"Here comes our favorite part of the chorus. When they sing, 'Make Mike the Tiger stand right up and roar. ROAR!' I lead everyone in a huge roar. They're playing my song!" Mike the Tiger says, as he runs into the middle of the action.

Mascot Message

Mr. C

Commodores
Home: Nashville, Tennessee
School Colors: Black and Gold
School founded in 1873

Ahoy there! What is a sea captain doing at a basketball game? It's Mr. Commodore cheering Vanderbilt to victory. Mr. C is usually dressed in a black and gold uniform but tonight, in Memorial Gymnasium, he is wearing his Memorial Maniac t-shirt. The

Memorial Maniacs are crazy fans of Vanderbilt basketball. Watch out if you get close to Mr. C at a game. "I often commandeer a little popcorn from fans who aren't looking," says Mr. Commodore.

Mr. C wears his

uniform every day. His black bicorne hat trimmed in white feathers makes people look. "I love the way the feathers on his funny hat wave back and forth when he moves his head," says one admirer. Bicorne hats, which are made by folding a wide brim up on each side of a hat, were stylish during the 1800s. An important part of the military uniform, Napoleon I wore this type of hat.

Napoleon I was a famous French military leader during the 19th century who almost took over the world. Does Mr. C want to dominate the world? "Only in basketball," jokes Mr. C. Like Napoleon, Mr. Commodore used to wear a sword with his uniform. "The sword got in the way during all my maneuvers," says Mr. C. "It is too hard to crowd surf if you are worried about your sword hurting someone so I put it in a safe place."

During football season, Mr. Commodore leads the Commodore Walk. The cheerleaders and band pump up the crowd as Mr. C marches the team along a star-spangled walkway to the stadium. At football games, Mr. C is in command as he patrols the sidelines supporting the team. He says, "Some people think I am very serious because I salute the crowd and often bend down on one knee for a better view of the game." Does he have fun at the games? He loves to crowd surf, which happens when fans lift him then pass him up and over their heads all the way to the top row of seats in the stadium.

When he is not cheering on his team, what does he do? "Academics first!" says Mr. C. "And I read everything about the sea. When I was a young swab-by, I loved *Treasure Island*. In fact, I've read *Treasure*

Island many times. I know good readers read their favorite books over and over." His best subjects in school are math and science. For exercise, he plays basketball but admits, "I am not nearly as good as the players on the teams."

Mr. C gets around. At Vanderbilt, you might see him at a baseball game in

the spring or touring the freshman dorms when school starts. He inspects the new students' dorms to make sure their rooms are shipshape.

During the summer, Mr. C attends mascot camp. One year, he went to mascot camp in Myrtle Beach, South Carolina. He and other mascots studied but also played on the beach and swam in the hotel swimming pool. What was his favorite thing about camp? "We planned and executed sneak attacks on the cheerleaders who were there, too," laughs Mr. C.

While he loves to travel to away games with his team, Mr. C says the best part of the voyage is seeing the beautiful Vanderbilt campus out of his porthole. The university is spread out over 330 green acres planted with more than 300 different types of trees and shrubs. In 1988, Vanderbilt was proud to be designated a national arboretum.

"The Vanderbilt Dyer Observatory is a favorite spot of mine," says Mr. C. "Located on top of a hill not far from school, it is the perfect spot for an old seadog to look at the night sky." He gets a closer view of those stars through its large telescope.

How did the Commodore become the mascot of Vanderbilt? In 1873, one of the richest men in the world gave $1,000,000 to start Vanderbilt University. This generous fellow was Commodore Cornelius Vanderbilt. At 16, young Vanderbilt started a ferry service between Staten Island and Manhattan in New York City. He made a fortune in the shipping and railroad businesses. He was nicknamed

"Commodore" because that is the title given to the senior captain of a line of merchant ships.

While Commodore Cornelius Vanderbilt was a serious man, Mr. C is a jolly guy who is friendly to everyone. He loves to pose for pictures so if you want his autograph or a photograph, just ask him. How can you spot Mr. C? He's the guy in the funny hat!

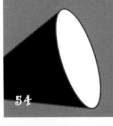

Mascot Message

Schoolwork comes first
Practice your skills and enjoy sports

Smokey

Volunteers
Home: Knoxville, Tennessee
School Colors: Orange and White
School founded in 1794

"Do I have any volunteers?" In the early 1800s, General Andrew Jackson asked this question when he needed soldiers to join the Tennessee militia. Many, many people rushed to duty, and Tennessee became known as the "Volunteer State."

The citizens of Tennessee and the students of the University of Tennessee have

continued to display this attitude. During World War II, for example, the university students decided to cancel homecoming. They sent the money they would have spent on the festivities to the Red Cross, which helps people who are in different types of crises.

When Tennessee was a frontier state, with unsettled lands stretching to the Wild West, Davey Crockett was a tough and heroic fighter. Today Davey Crockett is represented by the Volunteer, who leads the University of Tennessee fans and players to victory. It's easy to spot him on the sidelines in his coonskin cap, paying keen attention to the game's events.

But no outdoorsman is complete without a good dog, so the Volunteer is joined by the UT mascot, named Smokey. Smokey says, "When I was a young hound dog, I dreamed of joining the UT mascots, and even when the trail got tough I followed that scent until I was grown."

Smokey stays fit by jumping around and doing skits for the fans. With his long ears flopping, he uses his hound dog stamina to dance. He often sports a glittery jumpsuit in memory of another famous Tennessean, Elvis Presley. "I love wearing all my outfits, from my overalls to my orange suit, to this sparkly one. Watch this!" Smokey says as he spins around and does a split for the crowd.

In 1953, Tennessee fans decided to add a live Bluetick Coonhound to the mascot team. This breed of dog is native to Tennessee. During half-time at a football game, the Pep Club held a contest. Several hound dogs walked onto the football field. They put a microphone in front of each hound's mouth and listened to them bark. The last dog bayed the best.

"Even the fans joined in, and from that day on Smokey the Bluetick Coonhound has used his acute tracking powers to help the Volunteer and me hunt down victories for Tennessee," says Smokey.

Smokey loves the Bluetick Coonhound. "He's pretty small, but boy, can he howl!" They run and play until both dogs need a little rest. Smokey tries to keep the hound out of trouble. Smokey says, "Once, the Bluetick Coonhound tried to take on Baylor University's mascot—a *bear!*"

On home football game days, thousands of people enter Neyland Stadium, which has been enlarged or renovated 16 times. What are those boats out there? The Volunteer explains, "Oh, we call that the Volunteer Navy. Instead of driving here, they boat over. They dock on the Tennessee River right next to our stadium.

"It's crowded on the river, and it's also crowded at the Vol Walk," says the Volunteer. "Even people without tickets show up as Smokey and I wait on top of Peyton Manning Pass. We all walk down the hill, and the next time anyone sees us is when we run onto the field."

"We let our Bluetick Coonhound lead us onto the field," adds Smokey. "The band lines up in the shape of a humongous 'T.' We run right through it, past the orange-and-white checkered end zone to the middle of the field. I jump and dance, and the Volunteer waves the UT flag."

"Yep," adds the Volunteer, "I have to hold on to my cap during all this activity.

It's special because I made it from the skin of a raccoon I trapped. I run like lightning because the cheerleaders and the team are coming in right behind us!"

"Do you know what each football player does as he leaves the locker room?" asks Smokey. "On the way to the field each player touches a sign that reads, 'I will give my all for Tennessee today.' It reminds them to do their best."

Smokey and the Volunteer love the UT *alma mater*. They also enjoy singing 'Rocky Top.' "As soon as the Pride of the Southland Band plays the first note of that peppy song, the whole crowd joins in," says Smokey.

"Yeah," agrees the Vol. "Our opponents leave with 'Rocky Top' ringing in their ears."

The University of Tennessee mascots volunteer their time at just about any event that helps the people around them. Smokey says, "Hounds can cover a lot of ground, and I use my stride to get to all the sports events, charities, and some parties, too. I am a good-natured dog and I want to share myself with as many people as I can."

Mascot Message

Follow the trail and follow your dreams
It is important to volunteer to help others

Wildcat

Wildcats
Home: Lexington, Kentucky
School Colors: Blue and White
School founded in 1865

On game night, Rupp Arena is dark. Spotlights find the basketball players as they are introduced and run to center court. Fireworks pop in the rafters while smoke drifts down. Suddenly, the lights go up as blue and white streamers shoot to the floor. The students are on their feet screaming their favorite cheer, "C -A -T -S!" Who is standing in the eRUPPtion zone spelling "CATS" with his arms? It's the coolest cat around, the University of Kentucky's own Wildcat. He and his playful pal Scratch scat all over the arena whipping up support for their favorite team.

"Usually I am very relaxed but my fur gets riled up when the Cats are playing," says the Wildcat. "I have to go check them out and it doesn't matter if it is football, basketball, volleyball or gymnastics."

Scratch adds, "There is something about Big Blue that keeps me jumping like a cat on a hot sidewalk! We call our teams 'Big Blue' since blue is our school color."

With his blue baseball cap on backwards and smooth dance moves, Scratch is one hip-hop-happening kitty. He is the host of the Junior Wildcat Club for kids so he loves mingling with his favorite fans. But if you want to see him, you have to go to Lexington. Although he is a cat with attitude, he does not travel to away games. "I've got to stay close to home," meows Scratch the homebody.

The University of Kentucky has been known as the Wildcats since 1909. After a hard win over

Illinois, Commandant Carbusier, head of the military department, said the football team "fought like wildcats." Commonly known as bobcats everywhere else, wildcats are native to Kentucky where they are found mainly in the eastern part of the state. These medium-sized cats weigh up to 30 pounds and stand about two feet tall. Although they are shy, solitary creatures, wildcats are good hunters and can run as fast as 30 miles per hour.

"Sleek, strong, excellent leapers and able to take on Gators, Tigers and even Louisville Cardinals! That's why the Wildcats are a basketball powerhouse," purrs Wildcat. "So far, Kentucky's men's teams have won seven NCAA Basketball Championships and 25 SEC Tournament titles.

"I love everything about basketball games but my favorite moment is the Wildcat Pyramid. It has been called one of the greatest time-out moments in col-

lege basketball. An enormous white flag with a blue "K" on it is unfurled. Our band plays the theme from the movie "2001: A Space Odyssey" while the cheerleaders slowly build a pyramid. The crowd roars when I am lifted to the top of the pyramid. I pump my paws in the air and roar with them as the live pyramid slowly turns to face each side of Rupp Arena."

It sounds scary. Has he ever fallen? "Never! The guys who hold me up are really strong and careful. Besides, if I did fall, I guess that would just use up one of my nine lives," teases the Wildcat.

"UK Cheer is great!" adds his sidekick Scratch. "Our cheerleaders have won at least 15 National College Cheerleading Championships." One of his favorite moments during basketball games is when the cheerleaders spell out Kentucky. They lay on the arena floor and use their bodies as the letters. Someone special is always asked to make the 'Y.' Sometimes the Wildcat is honored to make the 'Y.'

During football season, the cats stay busy preparing for their Saturday antics in Commonwealth Stadium. Before each game, they rush to the stadium for the Catwalk. Along with fans and the cheerleaders, they yell encouragement to the players as they walk through a huge inflated helmet and into the stadium. During the game, the Wildcat does one-paw pushups every time the Cats score. One game, they scored so many points that the Wildcat did more than 500 pushups.

Cats that can spell and count? What an education they are getting! "My favorite subject is math so I can add up all the points during games," says the Wildcat. Energetic Scratch prefers PE. "I can't help it; I like to run around and play with the children at the games and pep rallies. That's why I always wear my blue hightops," yowls the kid-crazy cat.

What do they do in their spare time? "I love to sleep in my den. And I work out so I can stay fit for all those pushups I do. It's also fun to watch Scratch practice his dance moves while he admires himself in the mirror. You know, he thinks he's the cat's meow," jokes the Wildcat.

On, on, U of K! Go Big Blue!

Mascot Message

Exercise to stay healthy
Try something new every day